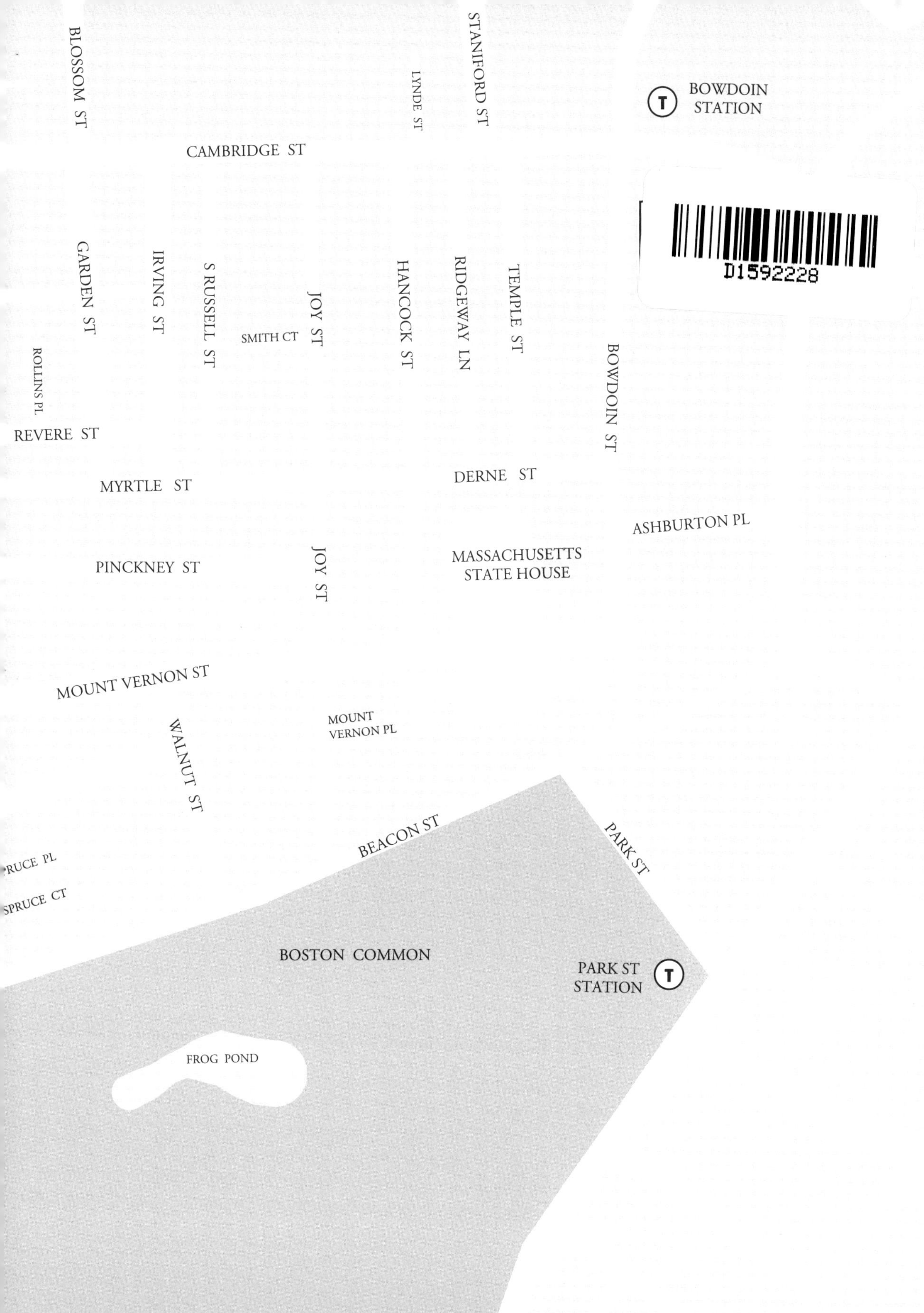
BLOSSOM ST
LYNDE ST
STANIFORD ST
BOWDOIN STATION
CAMBRIDGE ST
GARDEN ST
IRVING ST
S RUSSELL ST
SMITH CT
JOY ST
HANCOCK ST
RIDGEWAY LN
TEMPLE ST
BOWDOIN ST
ROLLINS PL
REVERE ST
MYRTLE ST
DERNE ST
ASHBURTON PL
PINCKNEY ST
JOY ST
MASSACHUSETTS STATE HOUSE
MOUNT VERNON ST
MOUNT VERNON PL
WALNUT ST
BEACON ST
PARK ST
SPRUCE CT
BOSTON COMMON
PARK ST STATION
FROG POND

Hidden Gardens of Beacon Hill

CREATING GREEN SPACES

IN URBAN PLACES

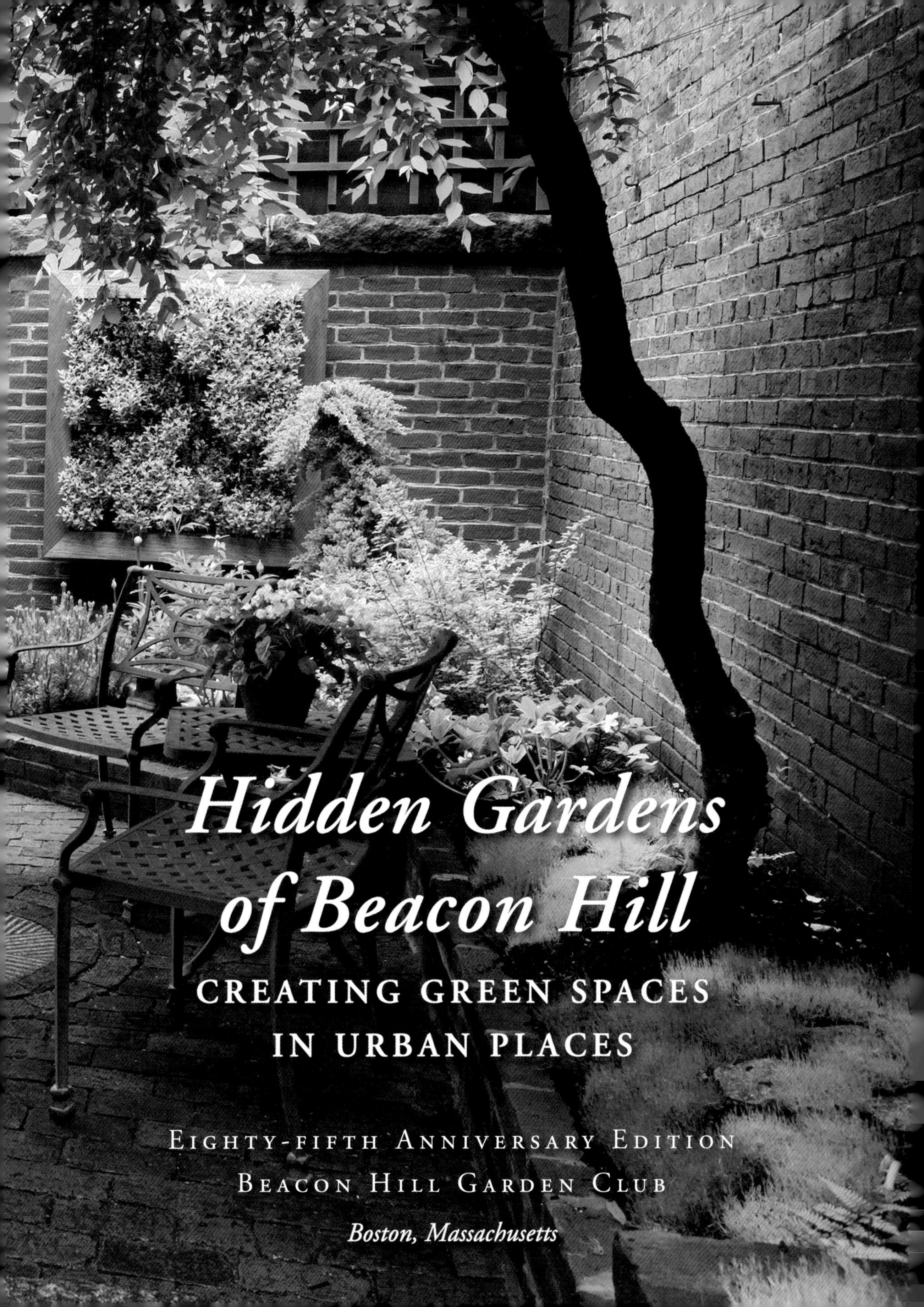

Hidden Gardens of Beacon Hill

CREATING GREEN SPACES IN URBAN PLACES

EIGHTY-FIFTH ANNIVERSARY EDITION

BEACON HILL GARDEN CLUB

Boston, Massachusetts

Hidden Gardens of Beacon Hill: Creating Green Spaces in Urban Places
Published in 2013 by the Beacon Hill Garden Club, Inc.
Box 302, Charles Street Station, Boston, MA 02114
www.beaconhillgardenclub.org

Beacon Hill Garden Club Presidents
Trudi Fondren, 2010-2012
Sharon H. Malt, 2012-2014

Beacon Hill Garden Club Book Committee
Jeanne Fiol Burlingame
Virginia Maloney Lawrence
Alexandra Marshall
Karen Cord Taylor
Eugenie L. Walsh

Primary Photographers
Tom Lingner
Peter Vanderwarker

Designers
Dede Cummings & Carolyn Kasper/DCDESIGN

Printing
PRINTED IN CHINA by Regent Publishing Services

10 9 8 7 6 5 4 3 2 1

Library of Congress Catalog Card Number: 2012954199
ISBN: 978-0-9887281-0-3

Proceeds from this book benefit local, state and national horticulture and conservation causes.

We dedicate *Hidden Gardens of Beacon Hill* to long-time club members Barbara W. Moore and the late Gail Weesner whose books have inspired ours.

Contents

SEVEN
BEACON HILL GARDENS
INCLUDING 3 NEW ONES
OPEN TO THE PUBLIC
THURSDAY, MAY 15th
(RAIN OR SHINE)
HOURS — 10:30 a.m. to 6 p.m.
TICKETS 99¢
ON SALE AT
FISHELSON, Florist 34 Charles St.
GUILD, Florist 31 Charles St.
PALLOTTA FLOWERS, Inc. 69 Beacon St.
and at the gardens:

EIGHT HIDDEN
BEACON HILL GARDENS
Open To The Public
THURSDAY, MAY 19th, 1977
10:00 A.M. to 6:00 P.M. (RAIN OR SHINE)

THE HIDDEN
BEACON HILL GARDENS
Open To The Public
THURSDAY, MAY 21, 1981
THE BEACON HILL GARDEN CLUB

THE HIDDEN GARDENS
OF
BEACON HILL
Open To The Public
THURSDAY, MAY 16, 1985
RAIN or SHINE, 9 a.m. - 5 p.m.
TICKETS $8.00 In Advance On Sale Now At:

The Hidden Gardens of Beacon Hill

THE
HIDDEN GARDENS
OF
BEACON HILL
OPEN TO THE PUBLIC
THURSDAY, MAY 18, 1995
RAIN OR SHINE, 9 a.m. - 5 p.m.

HIDDEN GARDENS
OF BEACON HILL
ANNUAL TOUR
Thursday, May 18, 2000
9:00 a.m. to 5:00 p.m., rain or shine

HIDDEN GARDENS
OF BEACON HILL
75th Anniversary Tour

Thursday, May 20, 2004
9:00 a.m. to 5:00 p.m. rain or shine
THE BEACON HILL GARDEN CLUB
Advance Tickets $25
Tickets on Tour Day (if available) $30
www.BeaconHillGardenClub.org

HIDDEN GARDENS
OF BEACON HILL
ANNUAL TOUR
Thursday, May 19, 2005
9:00 a.m. to 5:00 p.m. rain or shine

The Beacon Hill Garden Club invites you to the
Hidden Gardens of Beacon Hill
Annual Tour
Thursday, May 15, 2008
9:00am to 5:00pm
Rain or Shine
Advance $25 · On Tour Day $30
Tickets and Information Available Online
www.beaconhillgardenclub.org
or call 617-227-4392

Hidden Garden Tour
OF
The Beacon Hill Garden Club
Thursday, May 19, 2011
9:00am to 5:00pm • Rain or Shine
Advance $30 • On Tour Day $35
Tickets and information available online
www.beaconhillgardenclub.org
or call 617-227-4392

The Beacon Hill Garden Club
83rd Annual Tour of the
Hidden Gardens of Beacon Hill
Thursday, May 17, 2012
9:00 am to 5:00 pm · Rain or Shine
$30 In Advance · $40 Tour Day
Purchase tickets online & at Beacon Hill retailers.
For tickets and information, visit
www.BeaconHillGardenClub.org
info@BeaconHillGardenClub.org · 617-227-4392

Introduction

Drawing from the *Boston Evening Transcript, Saturday, May 18, 1929*

On September 26, 1928, twenty Beacon Hill residents, with a love of horticulture and a desire to see their small Boston neighborhood improved, met to form the Beacon Hill Garden Club. Gertrude Beals Bourne, a watercolorist who lived in the Sunflower House, at the corner of Mount Vernon and River streets, agreed to be president. Arthur D. Campbell of Pinckney Street became the temporary secretary and its long-time treasurer. Mary Cushman, or Mrs. Robert Cushman, as her name was recorded, of Mount Vernon Street, was named chair of the nominating committee. They were at work turning their own outdated laundry yards and service entrances into fine small gardens, and they realized the possible beauty and comfort such gardens could bring. In the spring of the next year they entered an exhibit of a small urban garden in the New England Spring Flower Show and also hosted the first Tour of the Hidden Gardens of Beacon Hill.

That first tour set the standard for all subsequent tours. The club opened eleven gardens in May, 1929, charged an admission price of one dollar and gave away the proceeds of $1,030 to horticultural and environmental groups. Since then the club has given away more than a million dollars raised through the annual tour and through the sale of its books, of which this edition is the fifth.

The Beacon Hill Garden Club has not forgotten the original members' intention to improve the neighborhood. In 1958 the club sponsored the Beacon Hill Window Box Project, giving prizes to the gardeners who beautified the neighborhood with the best window boxes. This contest, now sponsored jointly with the Beacon Hill Civic Association, has provided the stimulus for making window boxes iconic fixtures in this neighborhood, giving all residents the encouragement to do a bit of gardening whether or not they have a hidden garden.

Club members have also planted and taken care of four downtown Boston gardens. The Old North Church garden in the North End was planted in 1946, and the club has cared for it ever since. In 1993, working again with the Beacon Hill Civic

Historic photo of the Sunflower House garden of Gertrude Beals Bourne, the first president of the Beacon Hill Garden Club.

Association, the club transformed a recently installed traffic island at the intersection of Beacon and Charles streets into a horticultural oasis of gingko trees, shrub roses, bulbs and annual plantings.

Tree pits and window boxes are opportunities to beautify the neighborhood.

In 1994, club members noticed the abandoned playground and the crumbling entryway on either side of the old Peter Faneuil School building, which was being transformed into housing. They decided to do something about these eyesores. The largest of those gardens lies on the school's South Russell Street side. An honorary member of the club designed that garden, and the club arranged for its installation. It soon received the Garden Club of America's prestigious Founders Fund Award. The club continues to maintain this garden and its smaller sister garden on the Joy Street side of the old school. Club members also plant and maintain the long window box at the Charles Street Station Post Office at 136 Charles Street.

The club supports other non-profit organizations in their efforts to improve the environment and bring horticulture to urban spaces. We reserve a portion of the proceeds from our fund-raising activities for special projects, and recently have supported with significant funds the neighborhood's Tree Fund and projects initiated by the Friends of the Public Garden and The Esplanade Association.

To become a member of the Beacon Hill Garden Club, a neighborhood resident must have a hidden garden that is easily accessible to the public. Members are required to maintain their gardens in a delightful manner and open them periodically for the club's annual tour.

Through education, beautification and our fundraising efforts we provide Beacon Hill, Boston and the wider community with an increased appreciation of horticulture and an improved environment.

The Beacon Hill Garden Club is a member of the Boston Committee, the Garden Club Federation of Massachusetts and the Garden Club of America.

Character

Left: This garden is enhanced by the structure and formality of the brick basketweave and herringbone patterns and the Edwin Lutyens benches. The pear trees, Pyrus calleryana 'Chanticleer', have been cultivated to be narrower in habit and to withstand urban conditions.

Character

Right: Donald Wyman crabapple trees bloom at the same time that Chinatown tulips deepen to their darkest pink in this symmetrical garden.

Our gardens begin with constraints. In almost all cases we cannot change their size, the amount of sunlight they enjoy or their surroundings. It can be awkward and expensive to gain access to our gardens. Sometimes the only way to haul in compost is through the house. If we hire a tree removal company, the workmen do the work by hand. Our gardens simply cannot accommodate heavy equipment. And because our gardens are alike in their limitations they can seem repetitive.

Perhaps this is why we try extra hard to give our gardens a character of their own. Will the design be balanced or asymmetrical?

Playful or serious? Informal or formal? Modern or traditional? Some gardens back up to busy, noisy streets. Would it be better to design such a garden for viewing from upper windows rather than making it a garden in which to sit?

Will it have a Japanese theme, mimic an English country garden or evoke a woodland? Can it accommodate whimsy, strike an attitude or provide a contemplative setting? How can we introduce variety when we know that we'll have to rely on ivy, hostas, impatiens and climbing hydrangeas if we want to guarantee success? We address questions like these as we plan our gardens and as we adjust and alter them.

Above: The arched trellises reinforce the curves of the raised beds.

Right: An unexpected stand of birch trees creates this garden's woodland character.

This spacious garden has simple bones. Tall pedestals, low boxwood edging, a birdhouse and a ram's head fountain add complexity.

Our garden's character is determined by the elements we can't easily change: its structure, its levels and the materials of its walls, paving, gates and doors. Our choices of plants, ornaments, furniture, lighting and color provide comfort and pleasure and help us realize our garden's potential.

Throughout this book you'll discover the many solutions Beacon Hill's gardeners have arrived at to make our gardens appealing and useful.

Left: A rare sunny garden allows adults to watch children at play on the spacious terrace below.

Below: Horizontal layers of green provide a restful backdrop for a festive table.

Walls

Left: Several kinds of vines create a vertical landscape on the adjacent five-story building that overlooks this garden.

Walls

Right: Dutchman's pipe cascades over a wall of decorative arches.

Walls are what make our gardens hidden. It's not a deliberate desire on our part to conceal their presence. Walls do, however, create the boundaries within which we design. They provide privacy and determine the scale for each garden's ambitions. Most often, they are common walls, separating the spaces behind our brick townhouses but shared with a neighbor, and we can't change that situation. Sometimes a garden wall is the five-story building next door. In days of old, the walls were visual barriers, obscuring privies, laundry lines and the occasional horse stall.

Walls often block sunlight. They can be too high or too low. Invariably they are brick. If left unadorned a brick wall is devoid of interest. Over the years, we have come up with effective strategies to address this problem. In especially shady gardens, we often paint

Three treatments show examples of how we deal with walls. In one case, a slatted fence introduces more light and air. In another, a narrow garden uses a neighbor's wall to expand upward. In the third instance, an elaborate faux doorway adds a surprising element to a blank wall.

brick walls in light colors to brighten the space. We attach trellises, either natural wood or painted, to add color and texture. Such attachments may be strictly architectural features or may be intended for climbing vines. Sometimes the wall itself provides the support for vines.

Ivy is a reliable plant that will grow on a brick wall. Boston ivy turns red in the fall before its leaves drop. The tracery of its thin stems adds interest in the winter. English ivy is evergreen. Combining these ivies or mixing them with a Virginia creeper can add variety to a living wall. Such walls provide good cover for sparrow and purple finch nests.

In spring, wisteria vines display cascades of white, lavender or pink blossoms. In summer, climbing hydrangeas add flowers as well as foliage for pleasing visual impact.

When the garden is large enough, gardeners sometimes have installed wrought iron screens, segmenting the space while keeping it airy and open. Wooden fences, with their textures and colors, separate some gardens from the street and come in many imaginative forms, breaking the monotony of brick.

Some people believe that ivy harms the mortar in brick walls. Our experience has been different. Brick walls must be repointed every 50 years or so whether ivy grows on them or not. On Beacon Hill we like to say that the ivy is actually holding up our old walls.

Above: A painting enlivens a wall of latticework.

Left: Virginia creeper and ivy drape a wall. Beneath the fountain a healthy bed of European ginger forms a shiny base.

Paving

Left: Bricks laid in a herringbone pattern suggest movement and harmony, carving a path around planting beds that appeal to those looking out from the windows above.

Paving

Right: A colorful stone path contrasts with a traditional brick courtyard.

Bricks, bluestone, gravel, granite pavers, pebbles, slate, limestone, millstones and wooden decking provide the foundation for our gardens. In larger spaces these materials can be mixed and laid in patterns. In smaller spaces, a gardener may choose the uniformity of one material laid repetitively to visually increase the size.

The paving is a design feature that contributes to the character of the garden. This is especially important in that our gardens are seen from third- and fourth-story windows as well as from the ground level. Paving also enhances a garden's uses. Large slabs of bluestone may be best for families with small children who like to ride tricycles around. Gravel offers a crunch for gardeners wishing

Stepping stones float on a sea of gravel.

to introduce sound into the garden experience. Small granite blocks can be effectively used for edging or as a surface for a parked car.

Gardeners with long, skinny spaces often choose to install wider paving near their house for dining and then narrow the paving down to a path curving toward a focal point in the back wall of the garden. Sometimes trees or bushes on the sides of the path hide new features, revealing them pleasantly when one takes a stroll.

Sometimes paving is laid on top of soil. More often it is laid on crushed rock for drainage and covers dry wells and pipes that drain water from nearby rooftops.

We need paving because only a few of our gardens will grow grass. At least we are spared the drudgery of mowing. We sweep instead.

Granite pavers meet bricks in a curve reflecting the garden wall and the kitchen window.

Bluestone slabs set in a bed of stones make for a smooth walking surface.

Above: The paving in this garden acts as a carpet with year-round interest.

Left: White gravel is used to brighten this small, heavily shaded garden.

A zig-zag river of bluestone cuts between banks of brick edging.

Levels

Left: These levels take advantage of the slope of Beacon Hill to display a sophisticated arrangement of latticework, clipped boxwood and statues representing the seasons.

Levels

Right: Sometimes a garden lies above the lower level of a house. In this instance, the wide steps afford a graceful transition.

Beacon Hill rises sharply to almost 100 feet above sea level. As a result, our gardens are a form of terracing on pitched terrain.

At the Hill's steepest incline, two blocks down from the Massachusetts State House, a two-story formal garden is entered from below by a staircase built into a 12-foot high stone retaining wall. This unusually large and sunny garden is surrounded on three sides by tall neighboring buildings with fortunate views of its beautifully geometric trellised beds and the adjoining grassy square containing a round spouting fountain.

In gardens where the Hill slopes more gently, changes in level are accommodated with the installation of a step or two, or more, which can also permit us to divide the floor plan for multiple functions. With the use of plant material or decorative fencing, we create units of space to make the levels seem chosen rather than given.

Lower down, on the flat of the Hill, as locals call the land on the river side of Charles Street, we find that our gardens are often improved by installing subtle multiple levels to interrupt the smooth plane.

Above: Two sets of steps lead to a shared passageway running behind all the gardens on this block between West Cedar Street and Louisburg Square.

Right: The staircase in this 1811 granite retaining wall offers a spectacular approach to the sunny formal garden above.

Often, though, our gardens are neither horizontal nor vertical. We make our claims on the hillside with an artful variety of plant material designed to anchor the sloping land while providing lively horticultural interest. As a bonus, there is rarely a drainage problem since the rainwater makes its way downhill by virtue of gravity.

Above: The design of this garden incorporates subtle levels of terraces, steps and raised beds filled with woodland plants.

Right: A sitting area next to the house overlooks a cascade of circles and curves.

Gates and Doors

Left: A bold Z–braced door separates the public walkway from a private garden.

Gates and Doors

Right: An arched door is a lovely architectural feature leading to the lane beyond. Notice the peephole.

Beacon Hill's gates were originally built to permit deliveries of coal or ice or firewood into utility yards. Today they are used for the more modern convenience of unloading groceries or stowing bicycles. Our back gates may open onto a neighbor's front door across a common way, or lead to tunnels once understood as service entrances. A fortunate few homeowners come and go through garage doors that serve as the back wall of their gardens.

Since our gates are mostly wooden and square-cornered, adding an arch provides exceptional grace, and polished brass knockers and doorknobs are functional opportunities for decoration. Though discreetly locked, our gates are not forbidding. On the contrary, they were designed to offer entry.

Above: A wooden door offers easy access from a side alley to the garden and the kitchen door beyond.

Left and right: These gardens both use open arches in a fence to join two areas.

Doors leading from our homes into our gardens allow us to extend our lives into outdoor rooms for dining or play or for simple relaxation within the privacy of these planted enclosures. Our garden doors are often glass or mirrored to maximize light and expand the sense of space, not to mention making it possible, all year long, to enjoy close-up evergreen views.

Because our walled gardens can be entered either through doors that open out from the inside or gates that open in from the outside, as we come and go we are in effect using these doors and gates as transitions between our private and public lives. Sometimes, too, rather than merely passing through, we sense the beneficial effect of having this intermediate zone and are as glad for its send-off into the larger world as for its welcome back home.

Left: The open gates extend the design of the ornamental wrought iron fence.

Right: An open door reveals a straight path lined with privet and impatiens. At the end is an iron gate.

Below: This red door is a playful accent in a young family's garden.

Ornaments

Left: The ancient Buddha is from Thailand.

Ornaments

Right: A fountain with a child bearing a scallop shell birdbath is this garden's dominant feature.

We choose ornaments with great care. They must work well with the horticultural features of our gardens and provide interest twelve months of the year. They can supply a focal point. We see everything from an elegant statue prominently displayed on a pedestal to stone rabbits and squirrels tucked under ivy vines.

Deciding on the elements to place in our gardens allows us to express individual personality and style. Some ornaments are easily moved, so we use them to freshen up a design, change the mood, or introduce a new idea. They give us a chance to break the monotony of brick, especially when shade and poor air circulation limit the plants we can use. We sometimes have more space on our walls than on the ground, so we deploy hanging baskets to combine ornamentation with horticulture. With enough space, we include plaques, trellises, and troughs or fountains that give the pleasure of falling water and add soothing sounds to distract from the noise of the city.

This garden's many ornaments include a boy with a horn atop a fountain, trellises and an astrolabe flanked by large pots.

Containers offer our gardens the most flexibility and are ideal for growing herbs and small edibles. They can be placed on top of a garden wall to catch more sunlight than would be available on the ground.

A watchful mother duck with her ducklings surveys a garden enjoyed by the owner's children.

This garden is defined by ornaments, including an unusual pedestal as a table base.

We mark the seasons by changing sun-loving plants from tulips to roses to chrysanthemums as their blooms go by. As frost nears, we move containers inside to protect plants that are vulnerable to our New England winters.

Ornaments create conversation, surprise, entertainment and beauty. They are the urban gardener's accessories.

Right: A 17th-century English horse trough has a new life as a garden ornament.

Below: Craftsmen toil away on this stone planter.

This arrangement of handsome furniture invites conviviality.

Furniture

Furniture

Right: The dramatic design of the chairs adds an unexpected contemporary accent.

Not every garden is large enough to accommodate furniture. But when it is, it serves as another room where we dine al fresco, entertain during good weather, read the morning paper or provide a play space for our children and grandchildren. We consider not just function but aesthetics when we make furnishing choices. With limited space, furniture must be the right scale—no garden swings or massive wooden settees for us. Our options are tables, chairs, benches, and umbrellas. In most cases they are made of wood or wrought iron, natural or painted. But, increasingly, more contemporary furniture is being used to add variety to the traditional look of our gardens. Low walls offer additional seating.

Ideally, garden furniture combines comfort with a style that enhances the architecture of the house and garden.

Above: Pale green cushions offset the dominance of the brick.

Below: Café chairs and the French blue of the shutters suggest a bit of Provence.

Cushions and umbrellas afford opportunities to add comfort and color. Whether bright or subdued, color can complement the plantings and enliven an otherwise green palette. Because we have little storage space, our furniture stays in the garden throughout the year. Out of necessity it becomes sculpture, a feature especially appreciated when a bench or table is blanketed with newly fallen snow.

A wisteria, a Japanese maple and a Pieris japonica 'Mountain Fire' overhang the ornate wrought iron table and chairs.

Above: Curvy iron furniture brings femininity and grace to this garden.

Below: The tables and chairs in this shady garden add to the palette of greens provided by hostas, ivy, ferns and a stand of bamboo.

Above: Soft gray paint on the furniture suggests a gentle welcome to afternoon tea.

Below: A sculptural seating arrangement anchors this lush garden.

Dramatic outdoor lighting supplements the warm glow from the interior.

Light

Light

Right: This sunny garden allows for a greater variety of plants, including Japanese cedars and a Chinese elm.

The position of the sun, and the nearby buildings and trees that block it, determine the light in our gardens during the day. Some of us have a sunny spot during the entire growing season, but most of our gardens are shady. A successful magnolia or a Japanese maple can change the light available to adjacent plants as it matures. When we go to a garden center, we look for the plants that thrive in "Part Sun" or "Part Shade."

Pools of light dramatize features of this courtyard garden.

At night our gardens are lit by neighbors' windows, one of Beacon Hill's ever-burning gas lamps installed long ago in a walkway or beyond a garden wall, and by the lighting we build into the garden itself.

Lights can go along garden walls, under trees as uplighting, and around tree branches as twinkle lights. Lights can draw one's eye to a fountain or focal point. Candles protected from the wind are particularly nice on top of a wall or on an outdoor dining table. Lights can illuminate a path for safety and automatically come on when someone passes by.

Above: We bring light into our gardens with white walls or by using open-work screens instead of a solid wall.

Right: Wall lanterns illuminate snowflakes.

Even when we are not actually in the garden we can enjoy its lighting. Imagine sitting in a dining room during a summer rain having dinner with friends. The doors to the garden are open. The garden lights are on. The raindrops sparkle. The splash of the rain brings a sense of well-being since you are cozy and dry. Imagine lights illuminating snow.

Lighting our gardens at night can give pleasure not just to us, but to all the neighbors surrounding our gardens.

This ground floor seems brighter with a sunny garden outside.

Sometimes the only sunlight we get is dappled.

A courtyard makes up in color for what it lacks in size.

Color

Color

Above right: This urn is replenished periodically to add color throughout the seasons.

Below right: Pink and white is a common color combination in our gardens. Here, a Kousa dogwood and pink geraniums compliment each other.

Red brick and green shrubs, vines and ground covers dominate our gardens, most of which lie shaded by the five-story buildings surrounding them. It is a struggle to bring in color when most flowers need sun to flourish.

We cherish the flowering plants that can survive without full sun. That means we rely on impatiens, begonias and, increasingly, hydrangeas bred to tolerate a significant amount of shade.

Above: Two shades of blue at the rear of this garden add an unexpected backdrop.

Above right: Blue hydrangeas and white walls are a classic color combination.

Below right: The colors in the aptly named Sunflower House are balanced by the red Japanese maple and blue irises.

For more variety, we bring in potted plants, moving them to follow the sun as it changes position throughout the growing season, and replacing them when the shade finally ends their bloom.

We've found that light, bright colors—yellow, white and pale pink—show up best against the green background and the red brick walls. Plants with variegated leaves also show well, so many of our gardens have hosta and Solomon's seal with leaves edged in white. Clever gardeners introduce color by relying on furniture, cushions and other objects.

Above: An urban veranda is furnished with another example of the classic blue and white pairing.

Right: The brick color of the walls is repeated in the red tulips, a neighboring Japanese maple and the cushions on the chairs.

Spring is the best time to enjoy color in our gardens. In April and May such flowering trees as dogwoods, cherries and crabapples can grow tall enough to catch more rays than lower-growing shrubs and ground covers. In the fall we dig in dozens of daffodil and tulip bulbs rich with promise for the next spring's bloom.

Bluestone paves the garden proper while brick indicates the parking area. Decorative wood panels unify the two spaces.

Practical Solutions

Practical Solutions

Right: A tiered plant stand camouflages the bulkhead beneath.

Since the back yards of our houses were originally strung with laundry lines and used as outdoor kitchens and for privies, we can credit the gradual improvement in indoor plumbing, city services and household appliances for allowing us to inherit, and bequeath, the gardens of today. Nevertheless, our gardens must offer space for equipment and uses other than horticultural enjoyment.

A handsome antique occupies the parking space in this garden.

Handy parking is a rare and coveted benefit on Beacon Hill, so a few of our gardens have been divided to accommodate cars. Some gardeners camouflage their vehicles behind arbors of wisteria or climbing hydrangea. Once in a while, however, a vehicle becomes a kind of sculpture. Notable and charming is the 1929 Model A Ford, a beach wagon known as a "Woody," that graced the garden of an early member and has been displayed on tour day many times.

In addition, we make room for air conditioning equipment and for storing grills or firewood, trash barrels and garden tools. When not used for these practical purposes, original potting sheds have been refurbished into living space, sometimes with open decks above. In one such case, a decades-old carefully pruned Concord grape vine grows around the upper railing, yielding "City Grape Jelly."

While our children make good use of the Boston Common and the Esplanade along the Charles River for their play, some also enjoy gardens that accommodate

Coming and going can be challenging when the doors are not at garden level. Wide, sturdy stairs solve that problem.

A deck off the second floor serves as a slatted roof for the potting area below and as a support for masses of roses.

jungle gyms or sandboxes or baby pools, or offer enough room for tricycles. We encourage these future gardeners with pots of cherry tomatoes and herbs, or dedicate portions of the flower beds to planting pansies that can be repeatedly picked.

In an urban garden, where space can't afford to be wasted, we become inventive.

City kids play in their gardens in all kinds of weather.

The uniquely tranquil Annie Fields garden on this page and the next is enjoyed by occupants of the 14 surrounding buildings.

Shared Spaces

Shared Spaces

Right: This grassy oval is one of a kind on Beacon Hill, and is a perfect spot to visit with neighbors on a summer day.

While our gardens are hidden from the street, the description is somewhat misleading. Our gardens are, in fact, visible from beside, around and above, and we share their beauty with the neighbors who surround them. We share shade as our trees extend over our neighbors' backyards, and vice versa. We share such plants as wisteria, climbing hydrangea and trumpet vine, as they grow upwards and outwards, not confining themselves to our gardens.

At times plant wanderlust can cause problems. If shade or roots or invading plants are unwelcome, wise neighbors talk over the problem and seek a workable solution.

Some gardens are purposefully shared. One large open space exists behind 14 townhouses on the flat of the Hill. The neighbors,

Above: The Peter Faneuil House Garden was a gift to the neighborhood from the Beacon Hill Garden Club, and we continue to care for it.

Left: We share our gardens with wildlife, including a turkey who flew in for a visit.

Right: A narrow walkway leads to seven hidden gardens along its length.

some of whom are our members, maintain this garden, which is one of the rare gardens on Beacon Hill where a lawnmower is required. It is also a historic garden, planted in the 19TH century by the editor and writer Annie Fields, who lived in a house on Charles Street. Another shared space exists near the top of Beacon Hill. Originally this was one garden, but now two separate owners maintain two distinct areas, one with grass and the other with a symmetrical stone terrace.

Finally, the Beacon Hill Garden Club has designed and is caring for four public areas in downtown Boston. Our most precious shared spaces are the public parks and playgrounds that exist around our neighborhood. The Boston Common, the Boston Public Garden and the Esplanade along the Charles River serve as our front and back yards. We are proud of our financial support of these important green spaces.

Yews, boxwood, tulips and pear trees are a delight for the neighbors who overlook this magnificent garden.

Plants that succeed in our gardens

TREES

Birch *Betula*
Cherry *Prunus*
Corkscrew willow *Salix matsudana 'Tortuosa'*
Crabapple *Malus*
Dogwood *Cornus*
European mountain ash *Sorbus aucuparia*
Golden chain tree *Laburnum anagyroides*
Hemlock *Tsuga*
Honey locust *Gleditsia*
Katsura *Cercidiphyllum japonicum*
Magnolia *Magnolia*
Maple *Acer*
Pear *Pyrus*
Silverbell *Halesia carolina*

SHRUBS

Andromeda *Pieris*
Azalea *Rhododendron*
Boxwood *Buxus*
Bridalwreath *Spiraea prunifolia*
Cotoneaster *Cotoneaster*
Enkianthus *Enkianthus campanulatus*
Euonymus *Euonymus*
Firethorn *Pyrac antha coccinea*
Flowering quince *Chaenomeles*
Forsythia *Forsythia*
Holly *Ilex*
Hydrangea *Hydrangea macrophylla*
Juniper *Juniperus*
Laurel *Kalmia*
Leucothoe *Leucothoe*
Lilac *Syringa*
Mock orange *Philadelphus*
Privet *Ligustrum*
Rhododendron *Rhododendron*
Rose of Sharon *Hibiscus syriacus*
Slender deutzia *Deutzia gracilis*
Sweetshrub *Calycanthus floridus*
Viburnum *Viburnum*
Yew *Taxus*

VINES

Akebia *Akebia quinata*
Boston ivy *Parthenocissus tricuspidata*
Clematis *Clematis*
Climbing hydrangea *Hydrangea petiolaris*
Dutchman's pipe *Aristolochia*
English ivy *Hedera helix*
Honeysuckle *Lonicera japonica*
Mandevilla *Mandevilla*
Rose *Rosa*
Trumpet vine *Campsis radicans*
Virginia creeper or woodbine *Parthenocissus quinquefolia*
Wisteria *Wisteria*

PERENNIALS

Bellflower *Campanula*
Bleeding heart *Dicentra spectabilis*
Candytuft *Iberis sempervirens*
Chrysanthemum *Chrysanthemum*
Columbine *Aquilegia*
Coralbells *Heuchera sanguinea*
Dead nettle *Lamium*
Dutchman's breeches *Dicentra cucullaria*
Japanese anemone *Anemone hupehensis*
Lenten rose *Helleborus orientalis*
Lungwort *Pulmonaria*
Peony *Paeonia*
Primrose *Primula*
Rock cress *Arabis*
Speedwell *Veronica*
Violet *Viola*
Wormwood *Artemesia*

GROUND COVERS

Bugleweed *Ajuga reptans*
Hen and chickens *Sempervivum tectorum*
Myrtle or common periwinkle *Vinca minor*
Pachysandra *Pachysandra terminalis*
Plantain lily *Hosta*
Stonecrop *Sedum*
Sweet woodruff *Galium odoratum*
Wild ginger *Asarum*

BULBS AND RHIZOMES

Corydalis *Corydalis*
Crocus *Crocus*
Daffodil *Narcissus*
Grape hyacinth *Muscari*
Iris *Iris*
Lily *Lilium*
Lily of the valley *Convallaria majalis*
Ornamental onion *Allium*
Squill *Scilla*
Snowdrop *Galanthus*
Star of Bethlehem *Ornithogalum umbellatum*
Tulip *Tulipa*
Winter aconite *Eranthis*

WILD PLANTS

Barrenwort *Epimedium*
Christmas fern *Polystichum acrostichoides*
Cinnamon fern *Osmunda cinnamomea*
Cranesbill or wild geranium *Geranium maculatum*
False Solomon's seal *Smilacina racemosa*
Jack in the pulpit *Arisaema triphyllum*
Lady's slipper *Cypripedium*
Maidenhair fern *Adiantum pedatum*

Moss pink *Phlox subulata*
Partridgeberry *Mitchella repens*
Solomon's seal *Polygonatum biflorum*
Great white trillium *Trillium grandiflorum*
Wake robin or purple trillium *Trillium erectum*

ANNUALS

Begonia *Begonia*
Coleus *Solenostemon*
Geranium *Pelargonium*
Marigold *Tagetes*
Pansy *Viola tricolor*
Patient Lucy or Busy Lizzie *Impatiens*
Vervain *Verbena*

Beacon Hill Garden Club Active Members

The gardens of the active members of the Beacon Hill Garden Club are pictured in this book. See the page numbers beneath a name to locate a member's garden.

Sandra Ilgen, West Cedar Street
23 below

Elizabeth S. Ives, West Cedar Street
47 below

Rogina Jeffries, Brimmer Street
21 above, 39 below, 52

Elizabeth B. Johnson, Charles River Square
66, 67

Marty Keating, West Cedar Street
31, 78

Elena Kingsland, Pinckney Street
12

Joan Korb, Brimmer Street
19, 46 above

Virginia Maloney Lawrence, Pinckney Street
Cover page, 22

Sharon H. Malt, West Cedar Street
Title pages, 41 above

Alecia Ferris Manning, Pinckney Street
32, 57 above

Susan McWhinney-Morse, Temple Street
Dedication page, 14 below, 46 below

Lisa Meaders, Mount Vernon Square
11

Barbara W. Moore, West Cedar Street
44 below

Carolyn Morey, Chestnut Street
51 above

Katherine O'Keeffe, Chestnut Street
10

Paula O'Keeffe, Chestnut Street
53

Katie H. Ongaro, West Cedar Street
26

Carroll C. D. Pierce, Brimmer Street
4, 23 above

Lynne Rickabaugh, Pinckney Street
Half-title page, 42, 55 above

Sue W. Schenck, Louisburg Square
24, 33 below

Lynda A. Schubert, Chestnut Street
7

Molly H. Sherden, Walnut Street
30, 56

Kimberly Druker Stockwell, Chestnut Street
47 above

Lise Lange Striar, Pinckney Street
13, 34

Ann Sullivan, Chestnut Street
15

Karen Cord Taylor, Lindall Court
5, 59

Mary Frances Townsend, Chestnut Street
37, 62

Eugenie L. Walsh, Walnut Street
27, 35 above, 70 and 71

Amy Wilson, Mount Vernon Street
35 below

Additional members at time of publication:
Anne Almy, Caroline L. Bolter, Diana Coldren, Catherine Crowley, Arabella Dane, Katherine D. Flynn, Alicia Towns Franken, Cynthia Freeman, Deb Hanley, Natasha Hopkinson, Anne L. Jones, Susan Kearney, Joan Lee, Betsy Ridge Madsen, Alexandra Marshall, Nancy Mayo-Smith, Elizabeth W. McMeel, Nancy A. H. Mead, Louisa Paige Miller, Christy Nicholas, Kathryn O'Connell, Carolyn Osteen, Charlotte Patten, Ellen Plapinger, Rita Robert, Priscilla Ruegg, Jean D. Silver, Isabelle Storey, Nancy Tooke, Evelyn Liu Treacy, Jane Tyler and Sonja Yates.

Photographer Credits

Tom Lingner
title pages, dedication page, contents page, 4, 5, 6, 7, 10, 11, 14, 15, 16, 18, 19, 20, 21, 23 above, 24, 25, 26, 28, 29, 31, 32, 33 below, 35 below, 36, 37, 38, 39, 40, 41, 43, 44, 45, 46, 48, 50, 51 above, 52, 53, 54, 55 below, 57, 58, 59, 60, 61, 63, 64, 66, 67, 68 above, 78

Peter Vanderwarker
half-title page, 8 and 9, 12, 13, 17, 23 below, 27, 30, 33 above, 34, 35 above, 42, 47, 49, 55 above, 56, 70 and 71, 72, 76

Miroslav Bem
cover page, 22

Sun Ocean Photography ™
Caroline Townsend
page 62

A History of Beacon Hill

Throughout colonial times Beacon Hill was filled with marshes, pastures, and a few large estates such as the one John Hancock enjoyed overlooking the Boston Common. With the success of the American Revolution came self-government and the Commonwealth of Massachusetts. When early civic leaders decided to locate their new State House, completed in 1798, on the top of Beacon Hill, real estate speculators flocked to the surrounding hillsides. A new urban neighborhood was born.

Charles Bulfinch, architect for the Massachusetts State House and the U.S. Capitol, was one of the speculators who laid out handsome streets and planned luxurious estates with free-standing mansions. But their ambitions proved too extravagant, and they eventually settled on building large, four- and five-story brick rowhouses in the Federal style. Many of these early houses stand in the upper reaches of Mount Vernon, Chestnut and Beacon streets.

In the early 19TH century, city leaders decided to expand Boston. They cut off the top of Beacon Hill behind the State House, dumped the soil into the Charles River beginning at what is now Charles Street and gradually created the area we call the "flat" of the Hill. Meanwhile, sailors, bohemians, tradesmen and working class families were settling on the Hill's north slope, soon to be joined by a thriving middle class African-American community, who were then displaced by Eastern and Southern European immigrant laborers.

This early history created three different architectural styles in the neighborhood. On the south slope, real estate developers were in charge, resulting in more uniformity as the architecture changed subtly from the federal-style mansions at the top of the Hill into generally smaller Greek revival houses toward the lower elevations. The speculators were able to insert one lovely central garden into Louisburg Square, and they designed their streets so that few gave access to the less impressive north slope, causing today's Hill residents all kinds of inconvenience if they wish to drive around the neighborhood. Pinckney Street is a dividing line between the control of the real estate developers and the hodge-podge of individual tastes. That street has the most variety of styles of any street in the neighborhood.

The north slope grew up more organically than did the south slope, so it is on that side of the Hill that one finds little lanes, small walkways and surprising nooks and crannies. Some Greek revival townhouses survive on the north slope, but many of those structures were rebuilt into tenements around the turn of the 19TH to the 20TH century. Construction activity on the flat of the Hill extended mostly from the Victorian period through the colonial revival period of the early 20TH century. The flat has that era's townhouses and also has an eclectic variety of two- and three-story former stables and carriage houses, now converted into residences.

Charles Street serves as Beacon Hill's main street. That is where both residents and visitors find one-of-a-kind boutiques, antiques shops and such holdovers from an earlier day as an independent hardware store and drug store. The Hill's borders are perhaps the clearest of any of Boston's neighborhoods. Beacon Street is the Hill's south boundary. Storrow Drive is on its west. Cambridge Street forms the north boundary and Bowdoin Street its eastern edge, although new housing on that street and beyond is sometimes included in a definition of Beacon Hill.

The Hill's historic architecture is guarded by the Beacon Hill Architectural Commission, a state-sanctioned body that must approve all exterior changes visible from a public way.

Tour guides often describe Beacon Hill as a "tony" neighborhood populated by titans of industry. We do have residents who have made a name for themselves. But for most of the neighborhood's 9,000 or so residents, the Hill's most important aspects are its quirkiness, its livability, its convenience and its neighborliness. We share walls, roofs and front doors with one another. We know of one family whose furnace and laundry room are in their neighbor's building next door. We walk; we don't drive. Half of us don't even own a car. Stores deliver to us because no one can find a place to park to unload. New residents feel at home quickly as they get to know the shopkeepers and their neighbors through the many neighborhood organizations that are easy to join. Hill House provides many activities for families with children, and the nearby parks give kids plenty of places to play. Such conveniences and pleasures are hard to duplicate in other environments.

And finally, it's our gardens that keep us here. Surprising, even to us, as they display their changing seasons and as they attract birds, butterflies and a raccoon or two, they give us the natural beauty of a quiet space remote from the hustle and bustle of city life.

LONGFELLOW BRIDGE
CHARLES / MGH STATION
N GROVE ST
LINDALL PL
LINDALL CT
WEST CEDAR ST
WEST HILL PL
PUTNAM AVE
PHILLIPS ST
PRIMUS AVE
BELLINGHAM PL
SENTRY HILL PL
GOODWIN PL
GROVE ST
N
CHARLES RIVER ESPLANADE
CHARLES ST
CHARLES RIVER SQ
REVERE ST
MYRTLE ST
CHARLES RIVER
PINCKNEY ST
CEDAR LN WY
WEST CEDAR ST
LOUISBURG SQ
MOUNT VERNON SQ
BRIMMER ST
CHARLES ST
STORROW DR
MOUNT VERNON ST
ACORN ST
LIME ST
OTIS PL
BRANCH ST
BRIMMER ST
RIVER ST
CHESTNUT ST
BYRON ST
BEAVER PL
BEAVER ST
BEACON ST
BOSTON PUBLIC GARDEN
CHARLES ST
LAGOON